How Toys Work

Ramps and Wedges

Siân Smith

Heinemann
LIBRARY
Chicago, Illinois

www.capstonepub.com
Visit our website to find out more information about Heinemann-Raintree books.

To order:
Phone 800-747-4992
Visit www.capstonepub.com to browse our catalog and order online.

© 2013 Heinemann Library
an imprint of Capstone Global Library, LLC
Chicago, Illinois

All rights reserved. No part of this publication may be reproduced or transmitted in any form or by any means, electronic or mechanical, including photocopying, recording, taping, or any information storage and retrieval system, without permission in writing from the publisher.

Edited by Dan Nunn, Rebecca Rissman, and Sian Smith
Designed by Joanna Hinton-Malivoire
Picture research by Mica Brancic
Production by Victoria Fitzgerald

Originated by Capstone Global Library Ltd

Library of Congress Cataloging-in-Publication Data
Smith, Siân.
Ramps and wedges / Sian Smith.—1st ed.
p. cm.—(How toys work)
Includes bibliographical references and index.
ISBN 978-1-4329-6581-5 (hb)—ISBN 978-1-4329-6588-4 (pb) 1. Inclined planes—Juvenile literature. 2. Wedges—Juvenile literature. 3. Toys—Experiments—Juvenile literature. I. Title.
TJ147.S635 2013
621.8—dc23 2011041310

Acknowledgments
The author and publisher are grateful to the following for permission to reproduce copyright material: © Capstone Publishers pp. 5, 6, 8, 9, 10, 11, 12, 13, 15, 16, 20, 21, 23 middle bottom (Karon Dubke); Shutterstock pp.4 (© aquariagirl1970), 4 (© charles taylor), 4 (© Fesus Robert), 4 (© Phiseksit), 7 (© LIN, CHUN-TSO), 18 (© joingate), 19 (© Mike Flippo), 17 inset (© Daniel Taeger), 17 main (© SeDmi), 22 bottom left (© Mark Yuill), 22 bottom right (© Jiri Vaclavek), 22 top left (© c.byatt-norman), 22 top right (© macka), 22 middle top (© sarah2), 23 top (© SeDmi).

Cover photograph of a skater reproduced with permission of Getty Images (Photonica/Connor Walberg). Back cover photograph of a toy car on a ramp reproduced with permission of © Capstone Publishers (Karon Dubke).

We would like to thank David Harrison, Nancy Harris, Dee Reid, and Diana Bentley for their assistance in the preparation of this book.

Every effort has been made to contact copyright holders of material reproduced in this book. Any omissions will be rectified in subsequent printings if notice is given to the publisher.

All the Internet addresses (URLs) given in this book were valid at the time of going to press. However, due to the dynamic nature of the Internet, some addresses may have changed, or sites may have changed or ceased to exist since publication. While the author and publisher regret any inconvenience this may cause readers, no responsibility for any such changes can be accepted by either the author or the publisher.

Printed in the United States 4445

Contents

Different Toys 4
Ramps 6
Wedges 14
Quiz 22
Picture Glossary. 23
Index 24

Different Toys

There are many different kinds of toys.

Toys work in different ways.

Ramps

Some toys use ramps.

A ramp is like the side of a hill.

A ramp connects a high place and a low place.

Things can move up or down ramps.

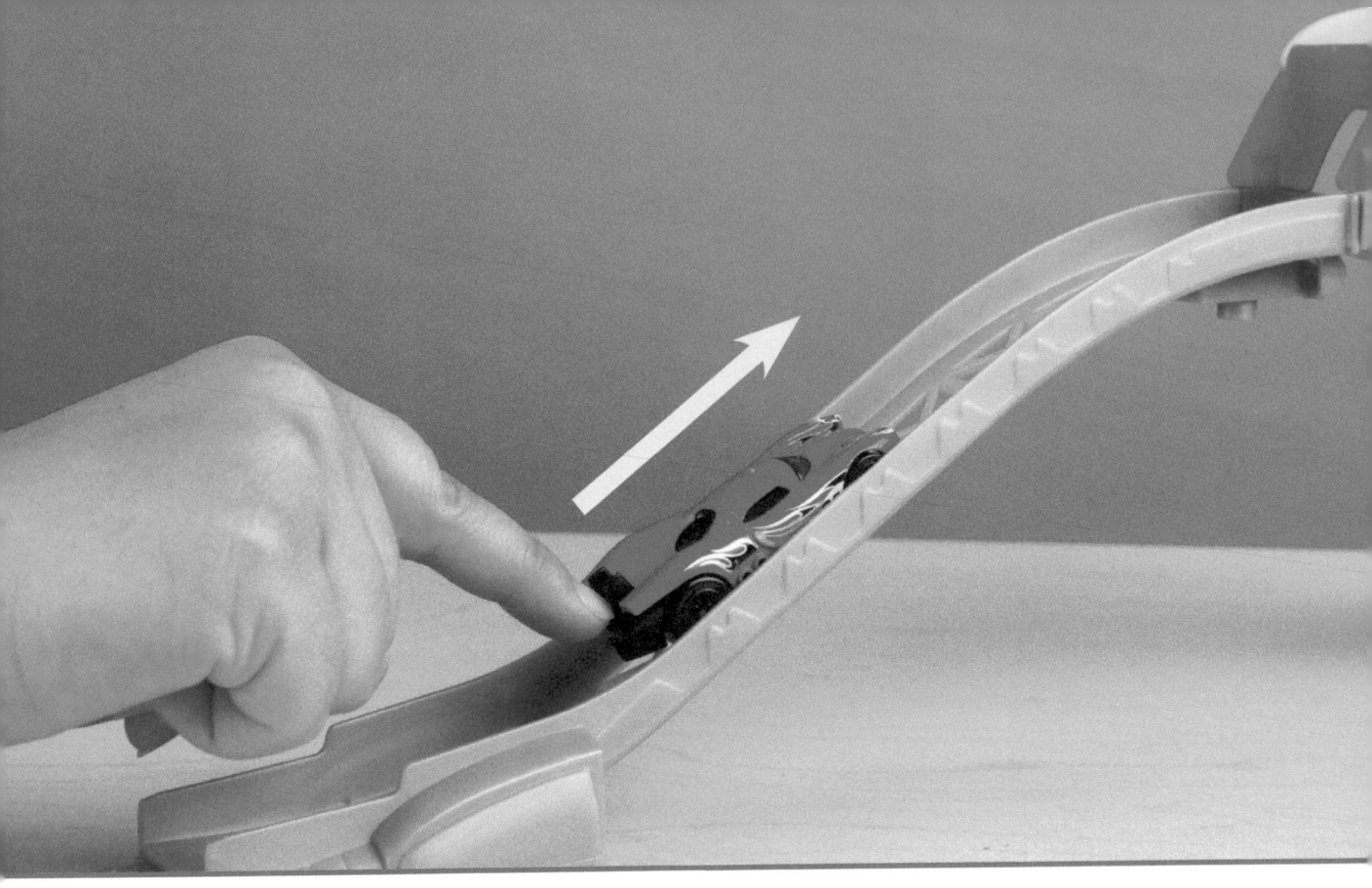

Things can move slowly when they are pushed up a ramp.

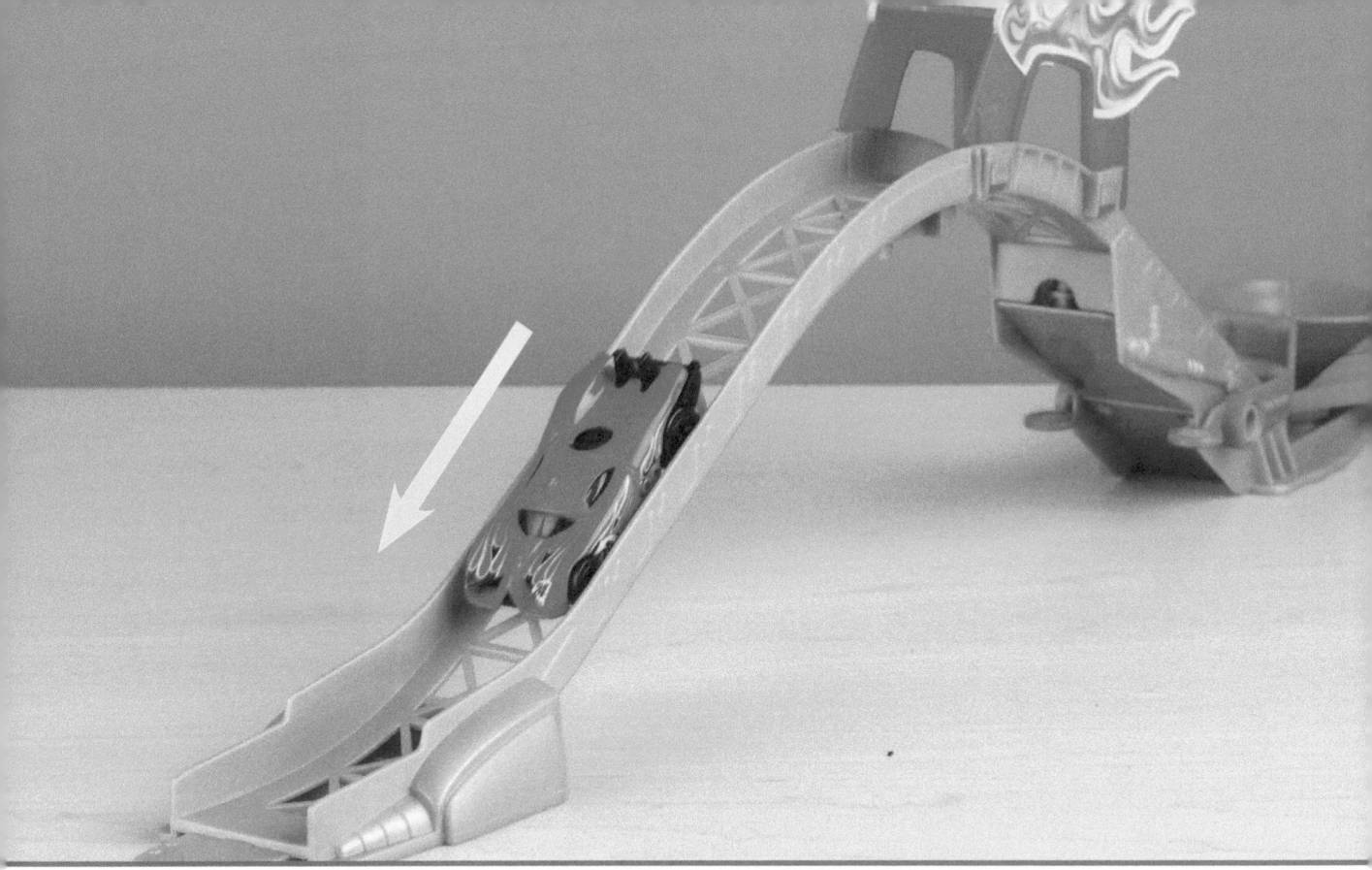

Things can move quickly when they are pushed down a ramp.

This marble run is a ramp.

This slide is a ramp.

Wedges

A wedge has a sharp edge or point.

We can push wedges into things.

Wedges can stop things from moving.

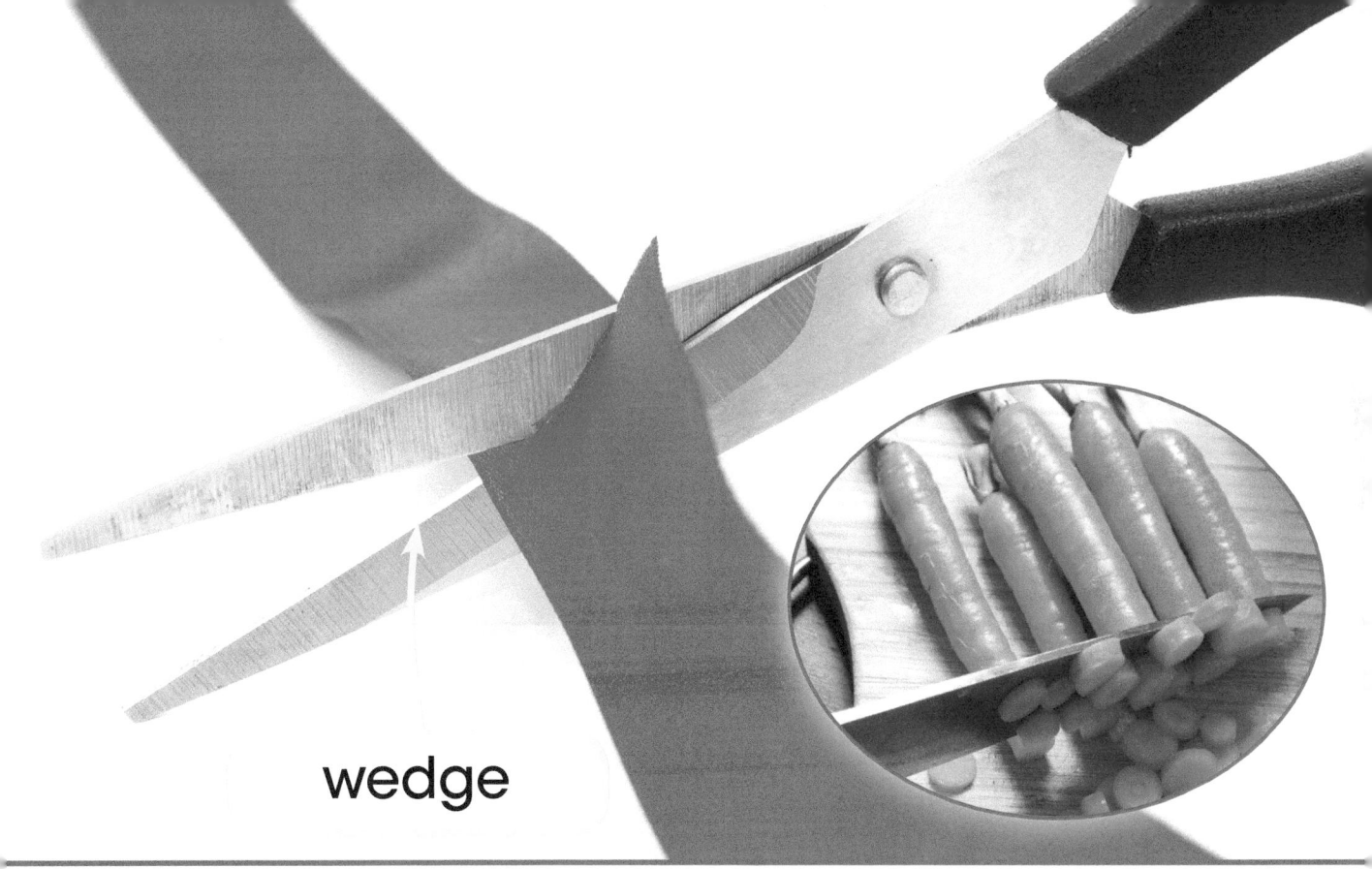

Wedges can cut things apart.

wedge

The end of this shovel is a wedge.

It pushes the sand apart.

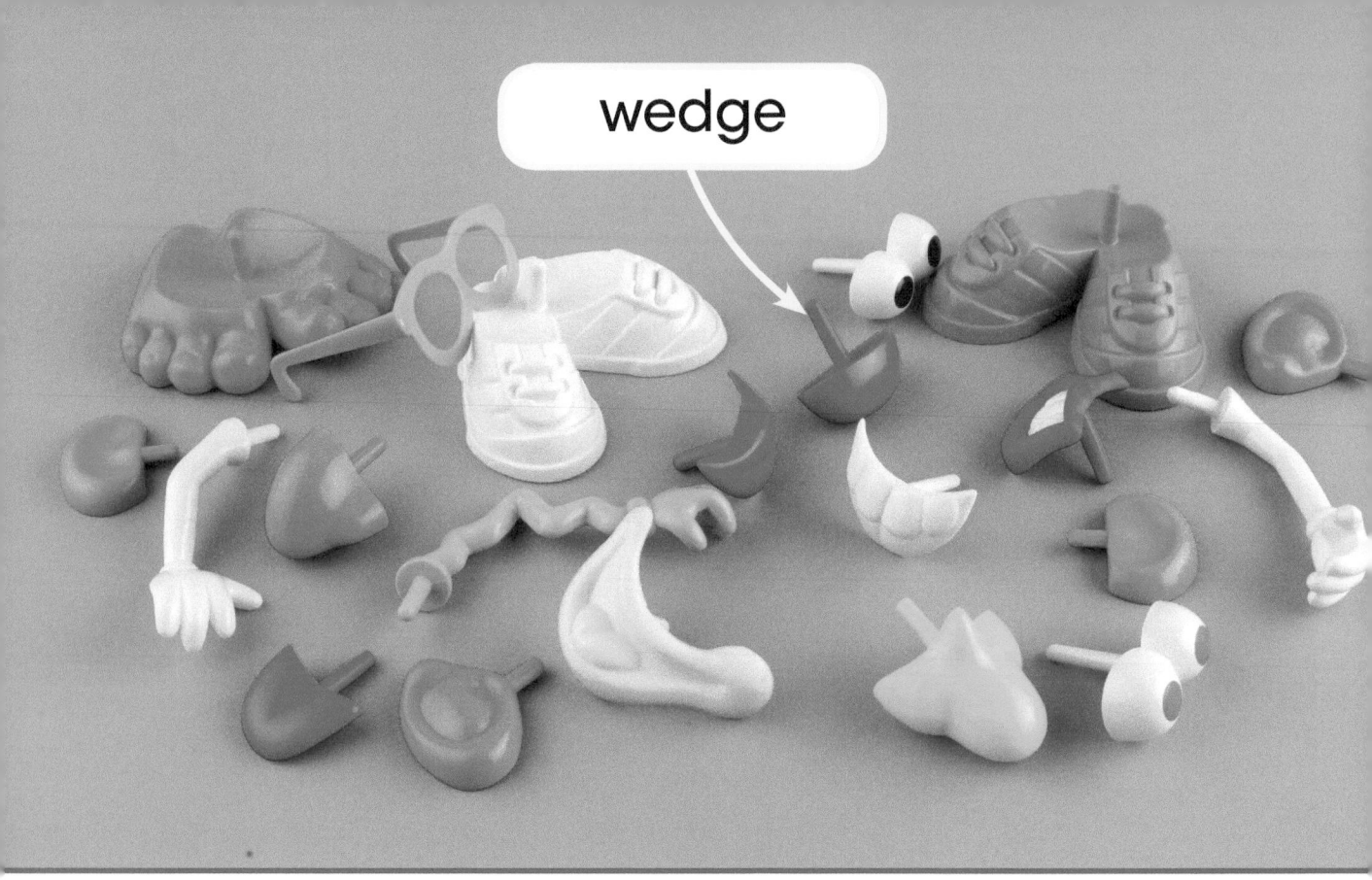

These toys have wedges.

You push them into the potato.

Quiz

a

b

c

d

Which one of these toys uses a wedge to work?

Answer on page 24

Picture Glossary

edge side of something. Some edges can be sharp.

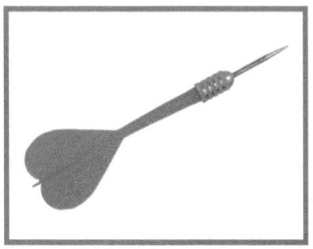

point sharp end. The end of a dart is a point.

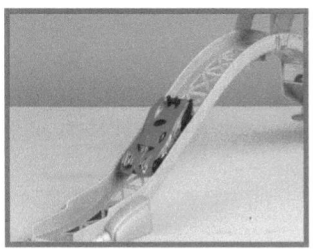

ramp a ramp is like a slope. It connects a high place and a low place.

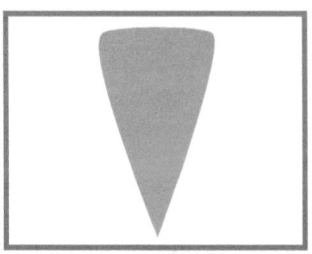

wedge piece of hard material with a sharp edge or point

Index

marble run 12
push 10, 11, 15, 19, 21
ramp 6–13
shovel 18, 19
wedge 14–21

Answer to question on page 22:
Toy b uses a wedge to work. A nail is a wedge.

Notes for Parents and Teachers

Introduce ramps

Show an example of a simple ramp. Explain that a ramp is like a slope that connects a low place and a high place. (Ramps are also called inclined planes.) It is easier to move something heavy from a low place to a high place if you use a ramp. Help the children to design and carry out an investigation using ramps. For example, investigate how far a toy car will travel if given a small push or big push down a ramp, or how changing the steepness of the ramp affects the distance it travels.

Introduce wedges

Show the children an example of a wedge—for instance, a plastic knife. Explain that wedges have at least one slanting side that ends in a sharp edge. We push wedges into things to split them apart. Knives, forks, axes, and scissor blades are examples of wedges. We also sometimes use wedges to keep two things separate and to stop them from moving.

Follow-up activities

Take the children on a trip around a school or home to find as many examples of ramps and wedges as you can. List, draw, or take photos of the examples you find. For more advanced work on simple machines, children can work with an adult to discuss and play the games at: www.edheads.org/activities/simple-machines.